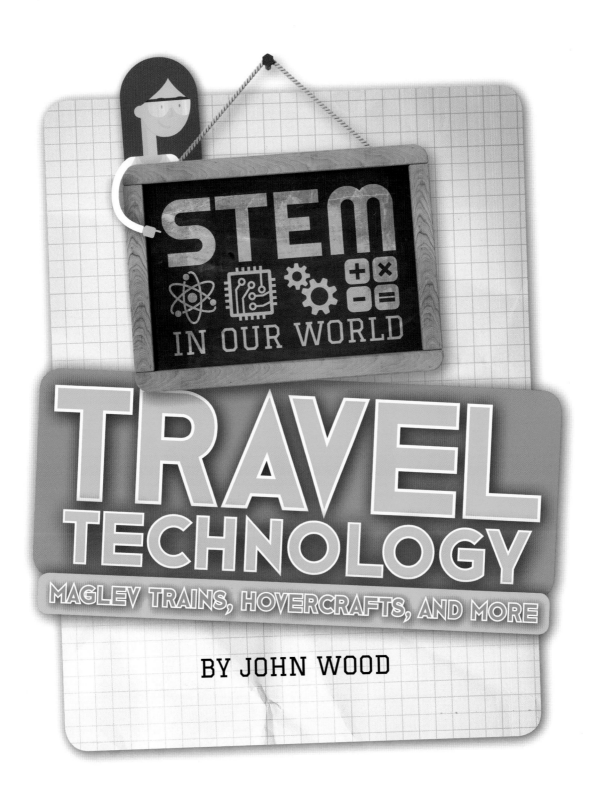

STEM
IN OUR WORLD

TRAVEL TECHNOLOGY
MAGLEV TRAINS, HOVERCRAFTS, AND MORE

BY JOHN WOOD

Gareth Stevens
PUBLISHING

Please visit our website, www.garethstevens.com.

For a free color catalog of all our high-quality books,
call toll free 1-800-542-2595 or fax 1-877-542-2596.

Cataloging-in-Publication Data

Names: Wood, John.
Title: Travel technology: maglev trains, hovercrafts, and more / John Wood.
Description: New York : Gareth Stevens Publishing, 2019. | Series:
STEM in our world | Includes glossary and index.
Identifiers: LCCN ISBN 9781538226551 (pbk.) | ISBN 9781538226544 (library bound) |
ISBN 9781538226568 (6 pack)
Subjects: LCSH: Transportation engineering--Juvenile literature. |
Motor vehicles--Juvenile literature. | Transportation--Juvenile literature.
Classification: LCC TA1149.W663 2019 | DDC 629.04--dc23

First Edition

Published in 2019 by
Gareth Stevens Publishing
111 East 14th Street, Suite 349
New York, NY 10003

© 2018 Booklife Publishing
This edition is published by arrangement with Booklife Publishing

Produced for Gareth Stevens by Booklife
Writer: John Wood
Editor: Kirsty Holmes
Designer: Daniel Scase

Printed in the United States of America

CPSIA compliance information: Batch #CS18GS: For further information, contact
Gareth Stevens, New York, New York at 1-800-542-2595.

CONTENTS

WORDS THAT LOOK LIKE **THIS** ARE EXPLAINED
IN THE GLOSSARY ON PAGE 31.

WELCOME TO STEM SCHOOL

ATTENTION, STUDENTS. MY NAME IS PROFESSOR TESS TUBE, AND I AM YOUR TEACHER. MY BUS DIDN'T SHOW UP THIS MORNING, SO I HAD TO USE MY JETPACK. UNFORTUNATELY, I SEEM TO HAVE... LOST CONTROL OF IT. FIDDLESTICKS. I'LL DEAL WITH THIS LATER. ANYWAY, I'M GLAD YOU'RE HERE. BY READING THIS BOOK, YOU ARE NOW PART OF STEM SCHOOL. STEM STANDS FOR:

ENTERING TURBO MODE

SCIENCE, TECHNOLOGY, ENGINEERING, AND MATH.

BUT STEM ISN'T ALL ABOUT RUNAWAY JETPACKS. STEM IS IMPORTANT IN ALL SORTS OF WAYS.

WHY IS STEM IMPORTANT IN ALL SORTS OF WAYS?

You can probably find STEM in almost every part of your life. Here are a few examples:

- COMPUTERS AT SCHOOL, WHICH HELP US LEARN
- TOASTERS, KETTLES, AND OVENS AT HOME, WHICH HELP US MAKE FOOD AND DRINK
- HOSPITAL MACHINES AND MEDICINE, WHICH HELP US LIVE LONGER
- CARS, BOATS, AND PLANES, WHICH HELP US TRAVEL AROUND THE WORLD QUICKLY
- WEATHER REPORTS, WHICH TELL US WHAT THE WEATHER IS GOING TO BE LIKE

Studying STEM helps us understand and solve problems in the real world. When we have an idea of how something might work, we test it again and again to make sure it is right. Then we can create machines and **SYSTEMS** to solve the problems we have.

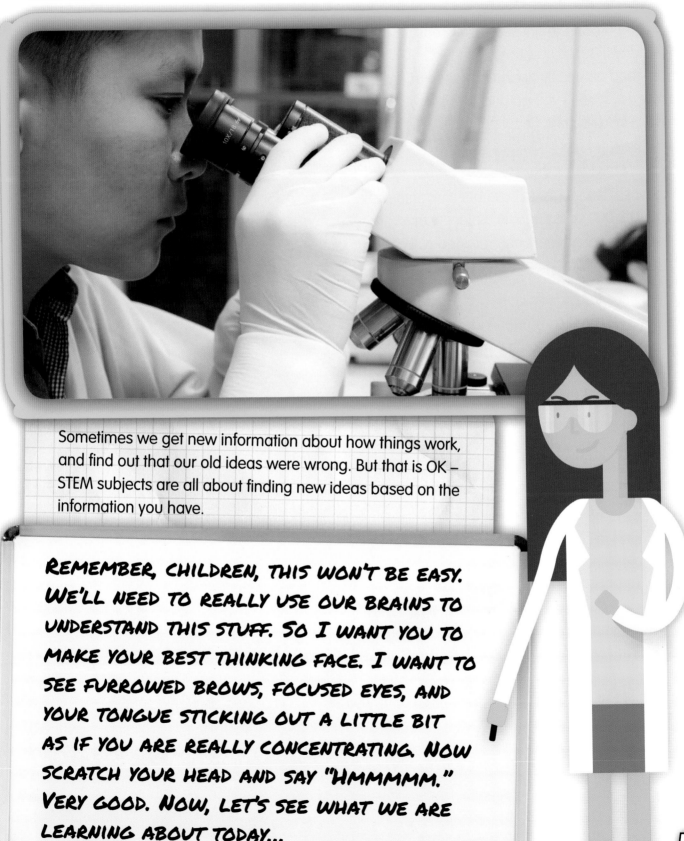

Sometimes we get new information about how things work, and find out that our old ideas were wrong. But that is OK – STEM subjects are all about finding new ideas based on the information you have.

REMEMBER, CHILDREN, THIS WON'T BE EASY. WE'LL NEED TO REALLY USE OUR BRAINS TO UNDERSTAND THIS STUFF. SO I WANT YOU TO MAKE YOUR BEST THINKING FACE. I WANT TO SEE FURROWED BROWS, FOCUSED EYES, AND YOUR TONGUE STICKING OUT A LITTLE BIT AS IF YOU ARE REALLY CONCENTRATING. NOW SCRATCH YOUR HEAD AND SAY "HMMMMM." VERY GOOD. NOW, LET'S SEE WHAT WE ARE LEARNING ABOUT TODAY...

STEM AND TRAVEL

TRAVEL BACK IN THE PAST

Traveling around might seem quite easy nowadays. Buses and trains connect cities, and planes fly across the world in a few days. But if you go back in history, it was very different. People have always needed to travel to be able to trade, make money, and learn from each other, but it used to take a very long time. Luckily for us, **TRANSPORTATION** has come a long way.

DISCOVERIES AND INVENTIONS IN TRAVEL

The wheel is thought to have been invented around 5,000 years ago, in a place that used to be called Mesopotamia (today this covers Iraq and parts of Syria and Turkey).

In 1804, Richard Trevithick built the first working steam locomotive. A locomotive is the engine of a train that pushes and pulls all the other carriages. Trains are good at transporting people and heavy things.

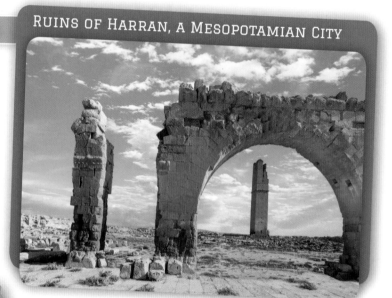
RUINS OF HARRAN, A MESOPOTAMIAN CITY

A RECONSTRUCTION OF TREVITHICK'S STEAM LOCOMOTIVE

In 1903, the Wright brothers successfully flew an airplane for the first time. Even though the flight only lasted 12 seconds, their invention led to the planes and helicopters that we see today.

THE FIRST AIRPLANE, BUILT BY THE WRIGHT BROTHERS

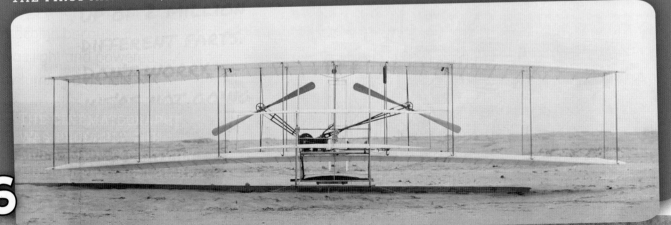

Progress is not slowing down for transportation. STEM research is literally speeding things up! New technologies and inventions are being discovered every day to make travel quicker and easier.

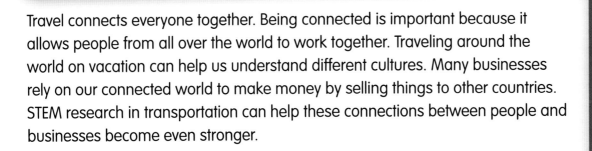

Travel connects everyone together. Being connected is important because it allows people from all over the world to work together. Traveling around the world on vacation can help us understand different cultures. Many businesses rely on our connected world to make money by selling things to other countries. STEM research in transportation can help these connections between people and businesses become even stronger.

BRRRRRRRIIII NNNNNGGGGG!

AH, THE BELL! IT LOOKS LIKE CLASS IS ABOUT TO BEGIN. ROLL UP YOUR SLEEVES, STUDENTS. WE ARE GOING TO TAKE A LOOK AT STEM IN ACTION. LET'S TURN THE PAGE AND SEE WHAT WE'RE GOING TO LEARN ABOUT FIRST...

MAGLEV TRAINS

FLOATING TRAINS
Maglev trains don't have wheels – they float above the track instead. They are safer, quicker, and better for the **ENVIRONMENT** than other trains. But how can a floating train be safer and quicker? To understand this, we need to learn about magnets.

A MAGLEV TRAIN IN SHANGHAI, CHINA

THERE ARE ALREADY MAGLEV TRAINS RUNNING IN SEVERAL COUNTRIES, INCLUDING CHINA, SOUTH KOREA, AND JAPAN.

MAGNETS: HOW DO THEY WORK?

THESE IRON FILINGS ARE SCATTERED INTO A PATTERN BY THE MAGNETIC FORCE. THE PATTERN SHOWS THE MAGNETIC FORCE LINES BETWEEN THE TWO SIMILAR POLES.

A magnet has two poles, called north and south. Poles that are the same **REPEL** each other and poles that are the opposite **ATTRACT** each other. If you've ever held two magnets together, you might have felt an invisible **FORCE** pulling them together or pushing them apart. Maglev trains use this magnetic force to make the trains hover.

ATTRACTING AND REPELLING

There are two types of maglev train:

- SOME TRAINS PUT OPPOSITE POLES NEAR EACH OTHER SO THAT THEY ATTRACT. THE TRACK IS SLOTTED INTO THE BOTTOM OF THE TRAIN. MAGNETS UNDER THE TRAIN ARE PULLED UP TOWARDS THE MAGNETS ON THE TRACK. THE TRACK'S MAGNETS ARE JUST STRONG ENOUGH TO LIFT THE TRAIN, BUT NOT TOO MUCH, OTHERWISE THEY WOULD STICK TOGETHER.

- YOU CAN SEE THE TRAIN AND THE TRACK SLOTTED TOGETHER IN THIS PICTURE.

- OTHER TRAINS PUT SIMILAR POLES NEAR EACH OTHER SO THAT THEY REPEL. MAGNETS ON THE TRAIN ARE PUSHED AWAY FROM MAGNETS ON THE BOTTOM AND SIDES OF THE TRACK, WHICH MAKES THE TRAIN HOVER.

Moving with Electromagnets

To move the train along, **ELECTROMAGNETS** are placed along the maglev track. Using electricity, electromagnets can reverse their poles or be turned on and off. The maglev train is pulled by the electromagnets in front of it and pushed by the electromagnets behind it. This is what keeps the train moving forwards.

MAGLEV TRAINS USE A SPECIAL TRACK.

The Secret Behind the Speed

When something moves, there are many forces acting on it. One of these forces is friction, which is the **RESISTANCE** between two things that rub together. You can feel friction when you drag something along the ground, and you can see friction working when a rolling ball slows down and stops. On a normal train, friction occurs between the wheels and the track. Maglev trains reach their high speeds because they are hovering, so there is less friction to slow them down.

JAPAN'S MAGLEV TRAIN CAN GO 373 MILES (600 KM) PER HOUR!

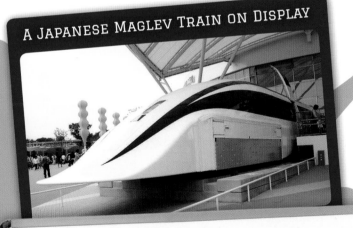

A JAPANESE MAGLEV TRAIN ON DISPLAY

HOWEVER, THERE ARE OTHER FORCES SLOWING MAGLEV TRAINS DOWN, SUCH AS AIR RESISTANCE. IN FACT, I THINK IT IS TIME TO LOOK AT THESE OTHER FORCES IN OUR NEXT LESSON: AERODYNAMICS! NOW, IF ONLY THERE WAS MORE AIR RESISTANCE ON THIS JETPACK...

AERODYNAMICS

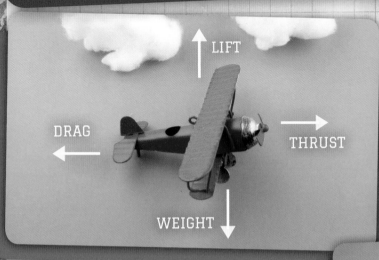

LIFT

DRAG

THRUST

WEIGHT

Aerodynamics is all about the different forces that act on an object as it moves through the air. There might be many forces acting on something at one time, often in different directions. When you add up all these forces, you can see how an object will move. Vehicles in the air deal with four main forces: weight, lift, thrust, and drag.

WEIGHT

Weight is the force that pulls the vehicle down. This is caused by **GRAVITY**. A heavier object feels a stronger pull of gravity, meaning the force pulling it down is much bigger. This is why heavier planes are more difficult to fly.

EVERYTHING WITH MASS HAS GRAVITY, INCLUDING YOU. HOWEVER, BECAUSE EARTH IS SO MASSIVE, ITS GRAVITY OVERPOWERS EVERYTHING ELSE.

THIS PERSON HAS JUMPED OUT OF A PLANE AND IS FALLING BECAUSE OF THE FORCE OF GRAVITY. LUCKILY THEY HAVE REMEMBERED TO PACK THEIR PARACHUTE.

LIFT

Lift is the force that pushes the vehicle upwards. For something to keep flying, the force of lift must be equal to, or greater than, the force of weight. Lift is usually created by wings or rocket engines.

THRUST

Thrust is the force that pushes the vehicle forward. Bicycles create thrust when someone pedals to turn the wheels. In a plane, the thrust is created by the engines.

DRAG

Drag is the force that pushes against an object as it tries to move. Drag is caused by friction between two objects, like wheels and the road. Drag can even be caused by the friction between the vehicle and the air itself, which is called air resistance. Air resistance is caused by air **PARTICLES** bouncing off the vehicle as it tries to move through the air.

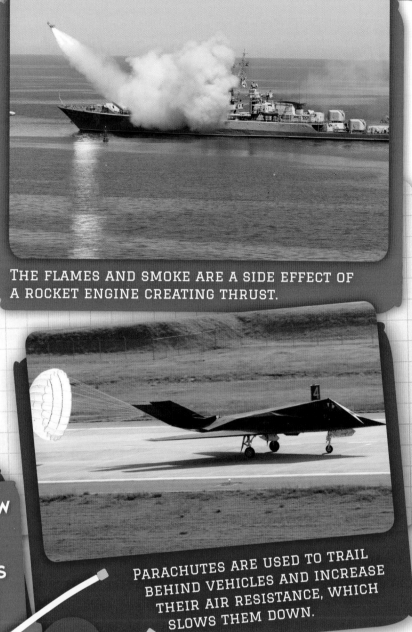

THE FLAMES AND SMOKE ARE A SIDE EFFECT OF A ROCKET ENGINE CREATING THRUST.

FAST VEHICLES HAVE NARROW AND POINTY FRONTS TO REDUCE SURFACE AREA. LESS SURFACE AREA MEANS LESS AIR RESISTANCE, OR DRAG, WHICH MAKES THE VEHICLE GO FASTER.

PARACHUTES ARE USED TO TRAIL BEHIND VEHICLES AND INCREASE THEIR AIR RESISTANCE, WHICH SLOWS THEM DOWN.

AS I FLY THROUGH THE AIR, GRAVITY PULLS ME DOWN AND AIR RESISTANCE SLOWS ME DOWN. LUCKILY FOR ME, MY JETPACK GIVES ME ENOUGH THRUST AND LIFT TO GO WHEREVER I WANT! AND THE PLACE I WANT TO BE IS THE NEXT PAGE, WHERE YOU'RE GOING TO BE LEARNING ABOUT AIRPLANES. SEE YOU THERE!

AIRPLANES

If you've ever wondered how those giant, metal planes can stay in the air as if by magic, then this lesson is for you. Hint: it's not magic.

AIR PRESSURE

The secret to flying is air **PRESSURE**. Air pressure is the force of air particles pushing against you. Areas of high air pressure have more particles, so there is more of a push. Areas of low pressure have fewer particles, so there is less of a push.

HIGH PRESSURE

LOW PRESSURE

AREAS OF HIGH PRESSURE WILL ALWAYS TRY TO MOVE TO AREAS OF LOW PRESSURE, SO THAT THE PARTICLES ARE SPREAD OUT EVENLY.

WING TECHNOLOGY

A plane moving through the air is a bit like your hand moving through water. The air flows around the plane like the water flows around your hand. To control the flow, the plane does two things:

- IT ANGLES THE WINGS SO THE FRONT OF THE WING IS HIGHER THAN THE BACK.
- THE WING HAS A SPECIAL SHAPE, WHERE THE TOP IS MORE CURVED THAN THE BOTTOM.

The air is split unevenly around the wing because of the angle and the shape. Most of the air particles go below, and fewer particles flow over the top. This means there is a lower air pressure above the wing.

THE WING IS HIGHER AT THE FRONT AND LOWER AT THE BACK.

The air from above rushes down to fill the area of low pressure. A fast, downward-facing flow of air is created, which runs down the top of the wing. Air particles also crash into the bottom of the wing, which pushes the plane upwards.

EQUAL AND OPPOSITE FORCES

Because the plane has forced all this air downwards, an equal and opposite force then acts on the plane, which forces it upwards.

Talking about equal and opposite forces might seem complicated, but you come across them all the time. For example, you can see equal and opposite forces when you go swimming. Your legs and arms push the water behind you, which makes you go forward through the water. The harder you push, the more force acts on you and the faster you travel. This is what the wings of a plane are doing. By forcing the air in a downward direction behind it, the plane moves in the opposite direction, which is upwards.

THIS DIAGRAM SHOWS THE SHAPE OF THE AIR AS IT FLOWS AROUND THE WING.

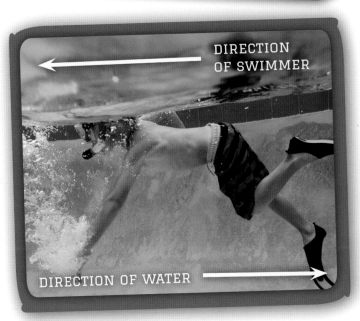

DIRECTION OF SWIMMER

DIRECTION OF WATER

DIRECTION OF AIR

DIRECTION OF PLANE

FLAPS ARE USED TO INCREASE THE SURFACE AREA OF THE WING. A BIGGER WING FORCES MORE AIR DOWNWARDS, WHICH CREATES MORE LIFT.

13

SOLAR-POWERED VEHICLES

SOLAR-POWERED VEHICLES CAN BE VERY EFFICIENT. THIS MEANS THEY USE SMALLER AMOUNTS OF POWER TO GO A LONG WAY.

SAEV

Solar-Assisted Electric Vehicles (SAEVs) are a type of electric car that get some or all of their power from the sun. Many countries are looking into solar technology and electric cars because they use clean, **RENEWABLE** energy from the sun.

STELLA LUX

Stella Lux is a solar-powered vehicle that will be taking part in the Bridgestone World Solar Challenge, which is a race between solar-powered vehicles in Australia. However, Stella Lux might become a car for anybody to use in the future.

Charged by the solar cells covering its roof, Stella Lux can travel 600 miles (965 km) on its battery, and has space for four people inside. It can also use its navigation system and the weather forecast to plan the best route in the sun.

STELLA LUX

THE PREVIOUS VERSION OF STELLA LUX, CALLED STELLA, WON THE BRIDGESTONE WORLD SOLAR CHALLENGE IN AUSTRALIA BACK IN 2013.

THE BRIDGESTONE WORLD SOLAR CHALLENGE? THAT'S A BORING FACT. I'VE GOT A MUCH BETTER ONE – IN AUSTRALIA THERE IS AN ANIMAL CALLED A WOMBAT WITH SQUARE POOP! GROSS AND WEIRD!

How Do Solar Cells Create Electricity?

Electricity is the flow of tiny particles called electrons. Particles can either have a positive charge or a negative charge. Like magnets, particles with similar charges repel each other while opposite charges attract each other. Electrons have a negative charge.

What Is a Solar Cell?

Solar cells are made up of two different layers; there is a negative layer, which has too many electrons, and a positive layer, which has too few electrons. These layers are separated by a *JUNCTION*.

SOLAR CELLS PRODUCE VERY LITTLE POWER ON THEIR OWN, SO LOTS AND LOTS OF CELLS ARE PUT TOGETHER TO FORM A SOLAR PANEL.

What Does Light Have to Do with It?

Light is a wave of energy. When sunlight hits the positive layer, it gives energy to the electrons. This extra energy makes the electrons jump up and move around. Sometimes, electrons can jump from the positive layer to the negative layer. However, this only works in one direction because the junction stops any electrons from jumping back. Instead, other electrons have to flow through a *CIRCUIT* to get to the positive layer and fill the space of the electron that has jumped. Whatever is attached to the circuit receives power as the electrons flow through on their way to the positive layer.

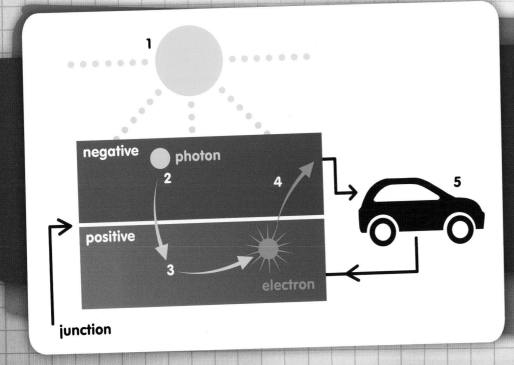

AS LONG AS THE SUN IS SHINING, ELECTRONS WILL ALWAYS BE FLOWING AROUND THE CELL AND THROUGH THE CIRCUIT IN ONE DIRECTION. THIS CAN CHARGE UP BATTERIES USED BY SOLAR CARS!

Check out my self-driving car! Look, no hands! No feet! And... no idea where it's taking me! Quick, learn how these things work so I can figure out what to do!

Right Around the Corner

Cars that can drive themselves already exist. They are able to avoid danger and safely get to their **DESTINATION**. When tested, self-driving cars are proven to be safer than cars driven by humans. Some self-driving cars are already being tested on our roads, driving alongside everybody else. Once it is decided that the technology is good enough, self-driving cars will be available to everyone.

A GOOGLE SELF-DRIVING CAR

AS OF 2017, GOOGLE'S SELF-DRIVING CAR HAS DRIVEN 4 MILLION MILES (6.4 MILLION KM) ON PUBLIC ROADS AROUND AMERICA. YOU CAN TAKE A RIDE IN GOOGLE'S CAR IN CERTAIN CITIES!

Better Than Humans?

Unlike humans, self-driving cars never get tired or distracted. They don't even need to blink. Not only that, self-driving cars would also drive in a way that would reduce traffic. All you would have to do is tell the car where you want to go, sit back, and relax.

SELF-DRIVING CARS MIGHT EVEN BE ABLE TO COMMUNICATE WITH EACH OTHER, SO THEY KNOW WHAT EACH CAR IS GOING TO DO.

How Does Google's Car Work?

Google's self-driving car has lots of sensors which tell the vehicle about its surroundings. Here are a few:

- CAMERAS THAT CHECK FOR PEDESTRIANS, TRAFFIC LIGHTS, AND ROAD SIGNS.
- **RADAR**, WHICH CHECKS WHERE OTHER CARS OR OBJECTS ARE. CARS ALREADY USE THIS TECHNOLOGY TODAY IN PARKING AND AUTO-BRAKING.
- AN AERIAL, WHICH PICKS UP **GPS SIGNALS** THAT GIVE THE CAR INFORMATION ABOUT WHERE IT IS.
- LIDAR, A ROOF SENSOR WHICH FIRES INVISIBLE LASERS IN ALL DIRECTIONS. THE CAR SENSES IF THE LASERS HIT ANYTHING, AND BUILDS A 3D PICTURE OF ITS SURROUNDINGS BASED ON WHAT THE LASERS FIND.

All of these sensors feed information into the car's computer. The computer has something called artificial intelligence, or AI for short, which means it can make its own decisions and think about what to do, just like a human would. The AI in the car is programmed to use the information from its sensors to decide what to do next.

HYPERLOOP

What Is Hyperloop?

At this moment, there is no working hyperloop system in the world. However, this technology may become a reality in the future. Here is the idea: a long vehicle called a **POD** would carry passengers through special tubes that are connected to different cities. A hyperloop pod would travel at high speeds, maybe as fast as 435 miles per hour (700 km/h). It would also be better for the environment than most trains and airplanes.

IN MAY 2017, THE FIRST TEST OF HYPERLOOP TECHNOLOGY WAS SUCCESSFULLY COMPLETED. FULLY WORKING HYPERLOOPS MAY BE OPEN TO THE PUBLIC IN 2020.

AN ILLUSTRATION OF A POD IN A VACUUM TUBE

How Would It Work?

No one knows for sure what technology hyperloop would use. Some people think that it would use technology similar to maglev trains, using magnetic forces to hover slightly above the ground. They might also use a small amount of compressed air to lift the pods. But this is not what makes hyperloop special. The real idea behind hyperloop technology is the special **VACUUM** tubes that the pods would travel in.

VACUUM TUBES

A vacuum is an area with nothing in it, not even air! Space is a vacuum but the sky is not, as it is full of tiny air particles. Hyperloop's vacuum tubes would have most of the air pumped out of them. The reason for doing this is the same reason for making the pods hover; to create less friction or resistance for the pod. If there are fewer particles of air to bump into, the vehicle will go faster because there is a lesser force of drag.

Many cities around the world, such as New York; Washington, DC; Dubai; and Abu Dhabi are currently deciding whether to build a hyperloop transport system. However, the cost of building the tubes is very high, so each city needs to decide if hyperloop is worth it.

WHAT DO YOU MEAN? IT IS EXPENSIVE, BUT I WANT HYPERLOOP NOW! WHO KNEW TUBES FULL OF NOTHING WOULD COST SO MUCH MONEY?

SUPERSONIC FLIGHT

Supersonic means faster than sound. Sound is a wave of vibration through something like air or water. When you clap your hands, you create a wave of energy that vibrates through the air particles. When this wave hits your ears, your ears turn the vibrations into sound and send it to your brain. To go faster than sound, you just need to go faster than that wave.

SOUND TRAVELS AT DIFFERENT SPEEDS THROUGH DIFFERENT THINGS. IT TRAVELS MORE SLOWLY THROUGH THE AIR THAN IT DOES THROUGH WATER. IT TRAVELS FASTEST THROUGH A SOLID.

MY NICKNAME AROUND HERE IS THE SUPERSONIC SCIENTIST BECAUSE I AM SO GOOD AT RUNNING. I AM ACTUALLY FASTER THAN SOUND, YOU KNOW. HOW FAST IS THAT? HMM, I'M NOT SURE BUT –

THE SPEED OF SOUND THROUGH AIR IS AROUND 1,125 FEET PER SECOND (343 M/S).

OH, UM, THANK YOU, COMPUTER. YES, THAT'S RIGHT, I AM QUICKER THAN 1,125 FEET PER SECOND. OK, LET'S MOVE ON –

THE SPEED OF PROFESSOR TESS TUBE THROUGH AIR IS AROUND 3 FEET (1 M) PER SECOND.

ALSO, PROFESSOR TUBE'S REAL NICKNAME IS THE SMELLY SCIEN-

ALRIGHT, ALRIGHT, THEY DON'T NEED TO KNOW MY REAL NICKNAME! I'LL NEVER LIE AGAIN!

SONIC BOOM

You may have heard of something called a sonic boom. Hopefully you haven't actually heard a sonic boom, because they are very loud. A sonic boom happens when a vehicle goes faster than sound: this is called supersonic. A vehicle pushes air in front of it as it moves forward, which creates waves of pressure in the air that spread from the vehicle. You can imagine this in the same way that ocean waves spread from a ship. If the vehicle becomes supersonic, it is moving so fast that the waves of pressure can't get out of the way. The waves bunch up together in one big, powerful wave. When this wave of pressure, or sound, hits your ears, you hear a loud bang!

AS PLANES GET NEAR SUPERSONIC SPEEDS, A WATER *VAPOR* CONE LIKE THIS ONE IS CREATED.

TODAY, THE SHAPE AND MATERIAL OF A PLANE STOP IT FROM BEING DESTROYED AT SUPERSONIC SPEEDS.

SUPERSONIC VEHICLES

Nowadays there are many planes that have the technology to be supersonic. Not only can these planes go very fast, but they are built out of very strong materials. This is so that they are not destroyed by the waves of pressure created at these high speeds.

21

ROLLER COASTERS

Theme Park Technology

Technology is making roller coasters faster and faster. The fastest roller coasters use similar technology to maglev trains. Electromagnets are used to power the roller coasters, and the bigger and more powerful the electromagnets are, the faster the roller coaster can go. But have you ever wondered how rollercoasters make people feel weightless? The answer has to do with gravity and inertia.

ALMOST...
GOT IT...

Inertia

Imagine being in a car when it goes through a roundabout. You may have felt pushed away from the roundabout as you go around it, especially if the car is going fast. This is because of inertia. Inertia is when objects keep moving as they were moving before. Something sitting still wants to stay still, and something moving in one direction will want to keep going in that direction. As the car turns around the roundabout, your inertia wants you to keep moving forward instead of turning. You need another force to **OVERCOME** the inertia.

THE PERSON IN THE RED CAR MIGHT FEEL PUSHED IN THE DIRECTION OF THE ARROW. THIS IS BECAUSE OF THEIR INERTIA.

You get this force by leaning or pushing against your seat belt or the car door. The seat belt or car door pushes you back equally, which gives you the force to overcome your inertia and turn with the car.

ON A ROLLER COASTER, IT IS YOUR SEAT OR SAFETY HARNESS THAT PUSHES AGAINST YOU.

THE FASTER YOU ARE GOING, THE BIGGER THE FORCE NEEDED TO OVERCOME YOUR INERTIA AND CHANGE YOUR DIRECTION.

FEELING WEIGHTLESS ON A ROLLER COASTER

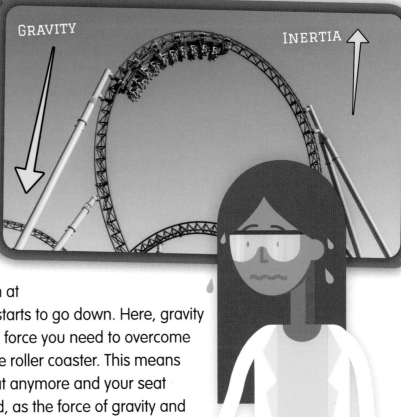

GRAVITY

INERTIA

The same thing happens on a roller coaster. When the roller coaster starts to go upwards in a loop, your body pushes against the seat to overcome your inertia and travel up with the roller coaster. When you are upside down at the top of a loop, the roller coaster starts to go down. Here, gravity is already giving you the downward force you need to overcome your inertia and travel down with the roller coaster. This means you aren't pushing against your seat anymore and your seat isn't pushing you back. For a second, as the force of gravity and inertia are balanced, you feel weightless – until you speed back to the ground, of course.

I CAN THINK OF ANOTHER FEELING I GET FROM A ROLLER COASTER. BUT, IF YOU DON'T MIND, I'D RATHER NOT GO INTO THE SCIENCE OF WHY WE PUKE ALL OVER THE PLACE RIGHT NOW.

HOVERCRAFTS

A hovercraft is a vehicle that can travel on both land and sea. As you might have guessed, hovercrafts hover over the ground a little bit. They do this by using a cushion of air. Hovering removes friction, which helps the hovercraft move.

AIR PRESSURE VS. GRAVITY

The hovercraft has a big fan in the middle which blows a lot of air under the main body of the vehicle, which is called the hull. The hull has a bendable skirt around the bottom, which traps most of the air underneath. As more air particles are trapped and squashed together, the air pressure increases. There is a greater push from the high air pressure under the hovercraft than there is from the lower air pressure above the hovercraft. If the air pressure is high enough to overcome gravity, the hovercraft is forced off the ground.

THE BENDABLE SKIRT IS USUALLY MADE FROM RUBBER.

HOVERCRAFTS USUALLY ONLY FLOAT A FEW INCHES OR CENTIMETERS ABOVE THE GROUND OR WATER.

IT'S TIMES LIKE THIS THAT I REALLY MISS MY HOVERCRAFT.

LAND AND SEA

A hovercraft only works on smooth surfaces. Smooth surfaces make sure the rubber skirt stays close to the ground at all times, which helps less air escape. If too much air escaped from underneath the hull at once, the pressure would go down and the hovercraft wouldn't hover anymore.

HOVERCRAFTS COME IN ALL SHAPES AND SIZES.

STEERING A HOVERCRAFT

THESE BACK PROPELLERS CREATE THE THRUST.

A second set of fans, mounted in the back of the hovercraft, blow air backwards and push the hovercraft forward. The direction of the air pushed behind can be changed, which also changes the direction the hovercraft is pushed. This is how the hovercraft travels in different directions.

BICYCLE FORCES

How Do Bicycles Stay Upright?

Mostly, bikes stay upright because the rider keeps them balanced. But there is a bit more to it, too. Bicycles are a surprisingly complicated piece of technology.

I DON'T UNDERSTAND THESE BICYCLES AT ALL. WHERE ARE THE ROCKET ENGINES? WHERE ARE THE LASER GUNS? NEXT YOU'LL BE TELLING ME THERE IS NO VOICE-CONTROLLED NAVIGATION SYSTEM.

You might have noticed that you don't ride in a perfect straight line when you ride a bike. You make lots of tiny turns and zigzags to keep the bike balanced, especially when you are going slowly. There is a reason for this. When gravity makes the bike and the rider fall to the left, we need another force to overcome gravity and keep the bike upright. We do this by turning the handlebars so that the bike turns left a little bit. Just like the passengers in the car on page 22, this causes the bike and rider to be pushed away from the left turn, which pulls the bike upright.

IN THIS PICTURE, THE FORCE OF GRAVITY PULLING THE BIKE DOWN TO THE LEFT IS BALANCED BY THE WOMAN BEING PUSHED AWAY FROM THE TURN, TO THE RIGHT.

But what makes a bike so stable and easy to ride? If you look at the diagram, you will see the steering axis. The steering axis is the invisible line that follows the bicycle fork. The trail is the distance between where the wheel touches the ground and where the invisible steering axis touches the ground. Having a bit of distance, or trail, means that the steering axis *ROTATES* as the bike leans. As the steering axis rotates, the wheel turns, which turns the whole bicycle into the direction it is leaning. So if the bike suddenly starts falling to the left, the wheel would automatically turn left. As we know, turning into the lean gives the bike enough force to overcome gravity and stay upright.

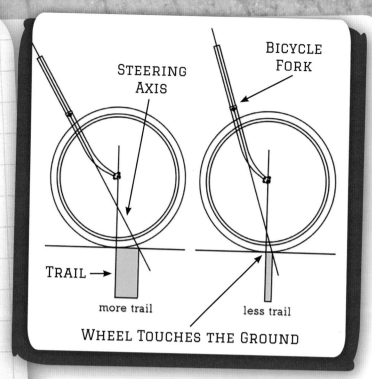

BICYCLE FORK

STEERING AXIS

TRAIL →

more trail

less trail

WHEEL TOUCHES THE GROUND

Bicycles were invented hundreds of years ago, and although they seem simple, there is a lot more going on than you think. Luckily, you don't need to know about any of this to actually ride a bike!

27

THE FUTURE OF STEM IN TRAVEL

Do you think you know what is going to happen in the future? Well, whatever happens, we are going to need lots of smart new scientists, engineers, and mathematicians. Here are some of the things that they might be working on...

Apps and Phones

Apps are going to become widespread in the future. Soon we will be organizing travel through apps all the time. This will be especially important with self-driving vehicles. Aside from the cars being developed by companies like Google, other self-driving vehicles include public transportation pods, which are also being tested today. These pods would be ordered through an app, and would be able to drive on the pavement and roads to get people around in a city.

Electric Cars

We already have electric cars on our streets today. However, in the future, all cars will probably be powered by electricity. Electric cars are more environmentally friendly, which is extremely important. In the future, cars that run on fuel, like gas and diesel, may be banned completely.

An Electric Car Charger

JETPACKS

There are plans to make real jetpacks in the near future. In fact, they are already being tested. The main use for the jetpacks will be for emergency services, like firefighters or police. The jetpack is powered by two fuel engines, and could be used to rescue people from small, hard-to-reach places where helicopters can't go.

A MARTIN JETPACK

DRONES

Soon your packages and mail will not be brought to you by a person in a truck. Instead, flying machines called drones will be used. Intelligent, quick and stable drones have already been created in **LABORATORIES** – in fact, drones have already been used to deliver a small package to someone in the English countryside. In the future, there may be thousands of drones buzzing through the skies, carrying mail. Companies hope that this will help orders be delivered in under half an hour.

CURRENTLY, DRONES MADE TO DELIVER PACKAGES CAN FLY AT 50 MILES PER HOUR (80 KM/H).

HOME TIME

THERE'S THE BELL. IT LOOKS LIKE ANOTHER DAY IN STEM SCHOOL HAS COME TO AN END. I SUPPOSE I SHOULD JETPACK HOME NOW.

`Fuel empty.`

UH-OH. COULD YOU POINT ME TO THE NEAREST JETPACK REFUELLING STATION? THERE ISN'T ONE AROUND HERE?! RATS. I'D BETTER START RUNNING FOR THE BUS. IF YOU LIKE STEM AND WANT TO LEARN MORE, THEN READ ON...

FIND OUT MORE

You could see if your school has any after-school STEM programs. Try talking to your teacher or your parents about how to get involved in STEM. You could also try thinking like a scientist, mathematician, or engineer yourself! STEM is all about solving problems – next time you see a problem, think about how it can be solved. You might be able to test your idea and see if it works. That is what STEM is all about.

FOLLOW THESE LINKS TO KEEP ON LEARNING ONLINE:

SCIENCE EXPERIMENTS
– www.funology.com/science-experiments

BBC SCIENCE
– http://www.bbc.co.uk/education/subjects/z6svr82

CRASHCOURSE SCIENCE VIDEOS
– www.youtube.com/user/crashcoursekids

GLOSSARY

ATTRACT pull or draw towards

CIRCUIT a path of wire that electricity flows through, which connects a power source to something that needs electricity

DESTINATION the place that someone or something is going to

ELECTROMAGNETS magnets that can be turned on and off using electricity

ENVIRONMENT the natural world

FORCE an invisible action, or reaction, between two objects that causes one or both to move

GPS SIGNALS signals from satellites that tell devices where they are or how fast they are going

GRAVITY the force that attracts physical bodies together and increases in strength as a body's mass increases

JUNCTION the point where two things are joined

LABORATORIES rooms or buildings that have the technology needed to perform scientific experiments

MASS the amount of matter that a body or object contains

OVERCOME become greater or more powerful

PARTICLES extremely small pieces of a substance

POD a detachable unit of a bigger vehicle

PRESSURE a continuous physical force exerted on an object, which is caused by something pressing against it

RADAR a technology that can sense the direction, speed, or presence of other vehicles

RENEWABLE able to be replaced through natural processes

REPEL push away

RESISTANCE the act or power of resisting or opposing someone or something

ROTATES turns around a central point or axis

SURFACE AREA the area of the outer of upper layer of something

SYSTEMS sets of things that work together to do specific jobs

TRANSPORT ways to get from place to place

VACUUM a space devoid of matter

VAPOR a substance in the gaseous state

INDEX

PHOTO CREDITS

Front Cover – maodoltee, Charlesimage, adike, xpixel, Marc Bruxelle, balabolka, mayrum. 2 – maodoltee, Charlesimage, adike, xpixel, Marc Bruxelle, balabolka, mayrum. 4 – Sira Anamwong, MaryValery, Jitlada Panwiset. 5 – toeytoey 6 – muratart, Ray Jones, Everett Historical. 7 – eldar nurkovic. 8 – JakeLM, MilanB. 9 – Chris 73, Gnsin, MaryValery. 10 – Berke, Mauricio Graiki, motive56. 11 – Alex Zabusik, Koalorka, MaryValery. 12 – pukach, Aris Suwanmalee. 13 – motive56, NadyaEugene. 14 – Arwel Parry, SolarEHV, Bjørn Christian Tørrissen. 15 – Diyana Dimitrova. 16 – Grendelkhan, graphic-line, Zapp2Photo. 17 – Grendelkhan 18 – u3d, chombosan 19 – TierneyMJ, u3d, NotionPic. 20 – Knot. P. Saengma, VVadyab Pico. 21 – Katerina_S, Jne Valokuvaus. 22 – MaryValery, derter, Lily Studio. 23 – ne3p, Stas Knop, VectorShow. 24 – Dave Turner, Vittorio Caramazza. 25 – MaryValery, Ivan_Nikulin, Thomas Philipp, Dean Clarke. 26 – Anna Grigorjeva, iskucctvo, Peter Snaterse. 27 – Matthew Grimm, sportpoint. 28 – Victority, Seksan 99. 29 – martinjetpack, Andrey_Popov. 30 – MaryValery, Rawpixel.com. Border on all pages: maodoltee. Graph Paper – The_Pixel. Tess Tube – mayrum. mages are courtesy of Shutterstock.com. With thanks to Getty Images, Thinkstock Photo and iStockphoto.